C0-AGV-891

NEW ARCHITECTURE IN BOSTON

NEW ARCHITECTURE
IN BOSTON

JOAN E. GOODY

THE M.I.T. PRESS

Massachusetts Institute of Technology
Cambridge, Massachusetts

Copyright © 1965 by
The Massachusetts Institute of Technology

All rights reserved. This book may not be reproduced,
in whole or in part, in any form (except by reviewers for the
public press), without written permission from the publishers.

Second Printing, April 1966

Library of Congress Catalog Card Number: 65-25273
Printed in the United States of America

FOR J-P BELMONDO

INTRODUCTION

Boston's large role in the early history of the United States and her rich heritage of buildings from past centuries are well known and well documented. So strong is the traditional image of this city that it may divert attention from what is happening today. But the mid-twentieth century is writing its chapter in the history of Boston architecture, and some of it is as deserving of study as anything in the past.

Recent architecture in Boston cannot be shown to be a development of any specific, local work of the past. This would seem impossible almost anywhere today when not only ideas but also architects travel widely and frequently. Some of the outstanding work here has been done by architects from other cities and countries, while buildings by Boston architects can be found around the world.

For the same reasons, there is no characteristic common to all the new architecture which could be called distinctively Bostonian. One of the interesting features of recent building in Boston is that it represents work by such a variety of architects, including Walter Gropius, Alvar Aalto, and Le Corbusier. This achievement results in large part from the emphasis that some of the educational institutions in the Boston area have placed on the architectural quality of their new buildings. The efforts made to choose a design for the new City Hall would seem to indicate that this concern has spread.

The structures presented in this book attempt to solve the problems of some aspects of the way we live today, using the most appropriate methods and materials from the broad range now available to us. Each of them stands out from the quantity of new construction in Boston by the kind of environment it creates for the activities it houses and by the way it affects its larger environment. Some of the buildings included are exceptional for the habitat produced; others are distinguished because of the way they adapt to and improve their surroundings, and some are successful in fulfilling both criteria. Each to a varying degree solves the functional problems efficiently, while bringing more than efficiency to the solution "by the way it encloses spaces and by the way it sits as an object in space" (Reyner Banham).

The photographs, drawings, and captions that follow are intended to point out the more noteworthy features of the projects as well as to help the visitor find his way to and around them. In anticipation of the book's use as a guide by those visiting the buildings, it has been arranged in roughly geographic order.

METROPOLITAN BOSTON

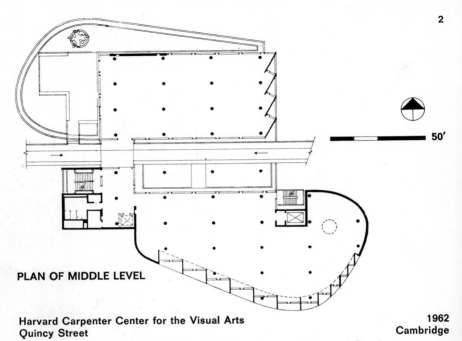

PLAN OF MIDDLE LEVEL

Harvard Carpenter Center for the Visual Arts
Quincy Street

1962
Cambridge

architect: Le Corbusier; collaborating architects: Sert, Jackson and Gourley

Adjacent to Harvard Yard, Corbusier's first structure in the United States is boldly pierced by a diagonal ramp that leads one through the major working areas of this sculptural building. Its roughly finished, largely undifferentiated studio spaces accommodate a flexible program of workshop courses in the visual arts for the undergraduates. There is a penthouse studio and garden for the resident artist who directs the Center's program.

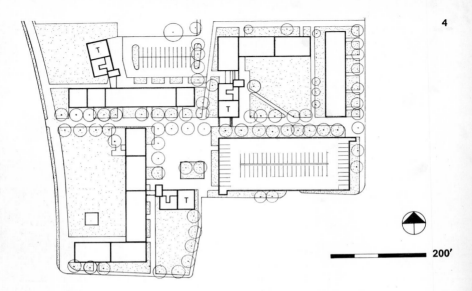

200'

Harvard Married Student Housing, Peabody Terrace
Memorial Drive and Flagg Street
architects: Sert, Jackson and Gourley

1964
Cambridge

In this project for 500 families, one basic unit (3 bays wide and 3 floors high) is used to form buildings of varied sizes and shapes around a sequence of paved and planted courtyards. To the motorist along the river, the changing relationships of the three 22-story towers are the focus of the group. But to the pedestrian passing through the series of plazas they enclose, the 3- to 7-story buildings are the important elements. These lower units (served by bridges from the tower elevators) also help to relate the new group in scale to the surrounding residential neighborhood and the older Harvard Houses.

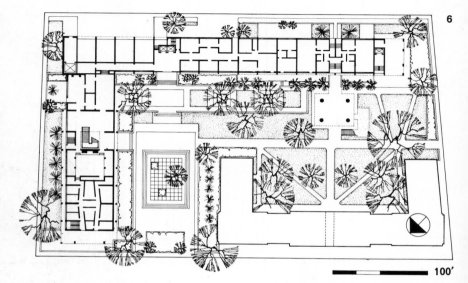

100'

Harvard Quincy House
Mt. Auburn and Plympton Streets
architects: Shepley Bulfinch Richardson and Abbott

1960
Cambridge

In the tradition of the Harvard residential halls, Quincy House includes a library, dining hall, resident tutors' facilities, and a Master's apartment as well as suites for the undergraduates. Unlike the older houses, the suites in the 7-story building are duplexes with all the living rooms (and the corridors) on the 3rd and 6th floors. Bedrooms and bath for each suite are up or down a private stair from the living-room floor, providing a separation of quiet and active ares. Another departure from the traditional buildings is the openness of the carefully landscaped courtyards enclosed by the house.

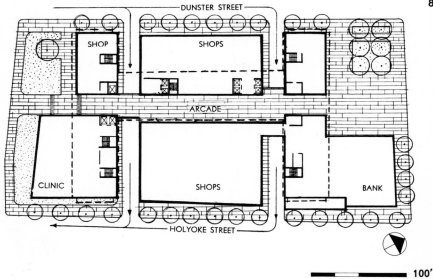

Harvard Holyoke Center
Mt. Auburn and Holyoke Streets
architects: Sert, Jackson and Gourley

1961
Cambridge

Built in stages, this project covers an entire block. A pedestrian arcade through the center links Harvard Yard and the Harvard Houses. Shops and open spaces alternate along the sides of the arcade. Above it a 10-story main building, containing offices, meeting rooms, and an infirmary, is H-shaped to allow light into the narrow side streets. Ramps from the street reach parking and service entries below the arcade level.

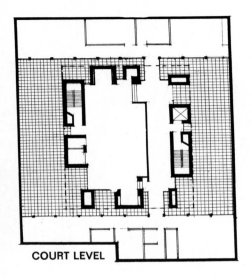

COURT LEVEL

TYPICAL FLOOR

50'

Harvard Graduate School of Education
Appian Way
architects: Caudill, Rowlett, Scott

1965
Cambridge

This 8-story building houses two quite different types of teaching space. Conventional classrooms with large glass areas line a sunken court at the building's base, while highly flexible interior space for the changing needs of graduate research programs are found on the upper floors. Stairs, utilities, offices, and other fixed spaces are placed along the perimeter walls, with windows located where required. This plan allows an open, central area that can be subdivided as necessary.

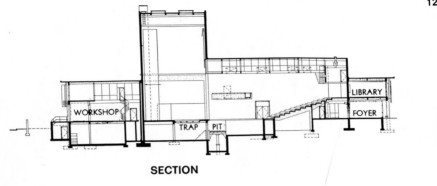

SECTION

50'

Harvard Loeb Drama Center
64 Brattle Street
architect: Hugh Stubbins & Associates, Inc.

1960
Cambridge

This building houses a theater that employs the most advanced mechanical and electronic systems of the stage technician, George C. Izenour, to control lighting, rigging, and seating. Its 359-seat conventional auditorium becomes an arena theater when the first seven rows split in two banks and pivot 90°, and a theater-in-the-round when they pivot 180°. Other facilities include a workshop, a try-out room, and a library. The lobby opens to a landscaped terrace.

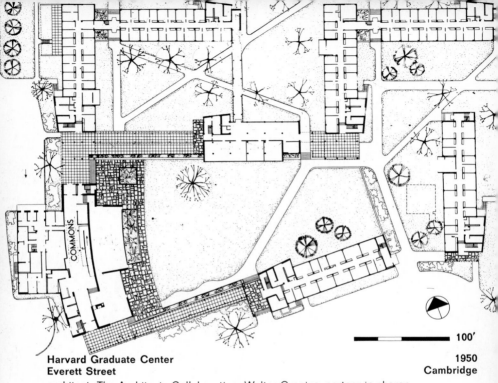

COMMONS

Harvard Graduate Center
Everett Street

1950
Cambridge

architect: The Architects Collaborative; Walter Gropius, partner in charge

These seven dormitories, the Commons building, and the covered passageways between them form a series of large and small quadrangles that are self-contained yet interlocking. The 3- and 4-story dormitories house 575 graduate students (in single and double rooms), and the Commons at the west end of the complex serves meals to 3000 students (1200 simultaneously).

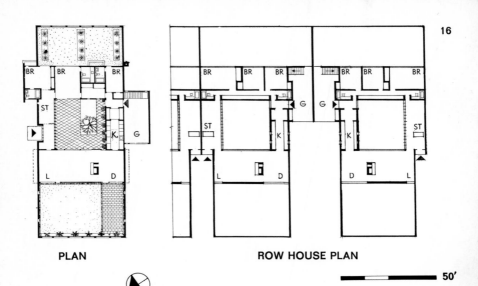

PLAN

ROW HOUSE PLAN

50'

Sert Residence
64 Francis Avenue
architect: José Luis Sert

1958
Cambridge

Built around a central patio, with fences extending to the lot lines enclosing additional front and rear patios, this city house obtains a rare variety of private outdoor spaces and controlled views. The placement of the large sliding glass doors gives views through the house from one court to another and a feeling of spaciousness. Although slightly modified for its specific occupants and location, the plan is a prototype intended for combination in rows and clusters on typical 60' x 100' urban and suburban lots.

ASH STREET

50'

Siple Residence
9 Ash Street
architect: Philip Johnson

1943
Cambridge

For this house, which Johnson designed for himself while studying architecture at Harvard, a small city lot was surrounded by a nine-foot high fence, and the rear portion roofed over. A glass wall separates the two sections thermally but not visually, producing a feeling of spaciousness in the small house and exposing the well-designed garden to the interior living area.

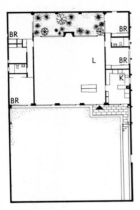

50'

Residence
1 Mt. Pleasant Street
architect: Paul Rudolph

1959
Cambridge

Located in the center of a city block, this house solves the problem of privacy of view and outdoor space with large glass areas facing the fenced-in garden on one side and a top-lighted conservatory on the other. Two bedrooms and the rear of the living room open to this densely planted, translucent roofed area. The house is a remodeled steel-framed garage with the original trusses left exposed and utilized to provide an unusually large, open living room.

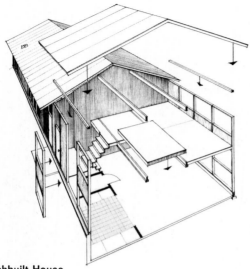

Techbuilt House   1958
23 Lexington Avenue   Cambridge
architect: Carl Koch & Associates, Inc.

This house is one of many variations based on a partially prefabricated, modular component system designed by Carl Koch in 1953 and currently produced by Techbuilt, Inc. While benefiting from some of the advantages of quantity production, the system provides a large degree of flexibility and adaptation to individual site and family requirements. The company provides a package for the basic house enclosure (including structural posts and beams, exterior wall panels, roof and floor panels) which is erected by a local builder. Interior partitions and finishes are supplied by the builder and, being independent of the exterior shell, they may be installed or rearranged to suit the occupants' different needs.

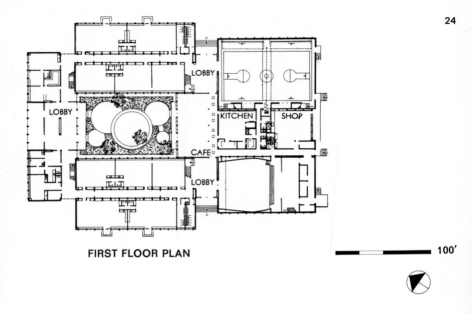

FIRST FLOOR PLAN

100'

Peabody School
Linnaean and Walker Streets
architect: Hugh Stubbins & Associates, Inc.

1962
Cambridge

This public elementary school for 600 students is located on a small site in an old, built-up residential area. Its compact plan works around a central courtyard where soft planting contrasts with the carefully ordered structural system expressed on the facades.

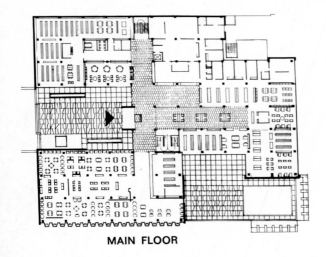

MAIN FLOOR

100'

Tufts Library
College Avenue
architects: Campbell and Aldrich

1965
Medford

The design for this 96,000 square foot library was chosen in a limited competition. The site is the steep slope of a hill overlooking Boston. In order to preserve the view from this important hilltop, which is the heart of the Tufts Campus, as well as to avoid overpowering the existing smaller buildings, the library is set into the hillside and its stepped roofs used as planting areas and terraces.

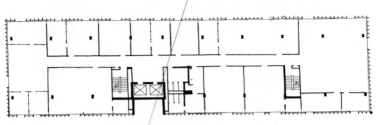

TYPICAL OFFICE FLOOR

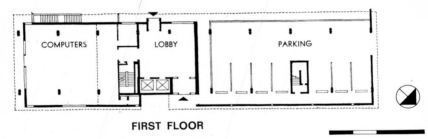

COMPUTERS   LOBBY   PARKING

FIRST FLOOR

50'

NEGEA Service Corporation
130 Austin Street
architects: Sert, Jackson and Gourley

1961
Cambridge

Housing the headquarters of the New England Gas and Electric Association, this reinforced-concrete structure has parking and computer facilities on the ground level, 3 floors of offices, and a cafeteria and executive offices on the top floor. The curtain wall facade of the building consists of precast concrete mullions spaced 2' 1" apart, and translucent glass sandwich panels. Clear glass viewing windows, from one to three spaces wide, are located in varying positions in each office.

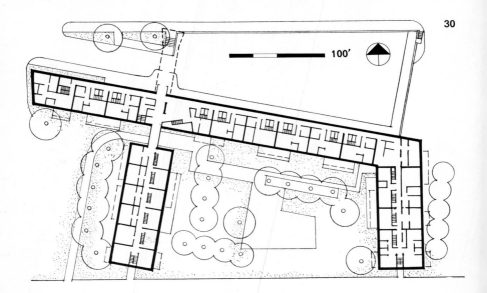

Eastgate Apartments
100 Memorial Drive

1950
Cambridge

architects: Carl Koch, William Hoskins Brown, Robert Woods Kennedy,
Vernon De Mars, Ralph Rapson

Due to its siting and elevator system, this 12-story building is able to provide each of the 261 apartments with a balcony or terrace, a view of the river, and direct sunlight. This is accomplished economically by having the elevator stop at only every third floor, where a corridor runs along the north side and private stairs go up and down to through apartments on the other floors. Common facilities include a penthouse laundry and community room and a small store.

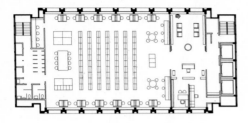

LIBRARY FLOOR

50′

M.I.T. Cecil and Ida Green Building
East Campus, Near Ames Street
architects: I. M. Pei & Associates

1964
Cambridge

Although an abrupt departure from the low plateau of buildings that surround it, this 23-story tower is linked to the original M.I.T. structures by its dignified form and the color and texture of its concrete facing material. Solid side walls give the tall building stiffness against the wind as well as house the ducts and pipes required for the laboratories. The window walls are load bearing and thus allow column-free floor space.

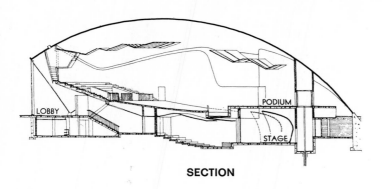

SECTION

50′

M.I.T. Kresge Auditorium   1955
West Campus, Massachusetts Avenue   Cambridge
architect: Eero Saarinen; associate architects: Anderson, Beckwith and Haible

The thin-shelled concrete dome that covers this auditorium, only 3½″ thick at its apogee, was thought by its architect to be "appropriate to express the spirit" of a school of technology and is also appropriate for a school whose architecture is characterized by two other important domes. Within the space enclosed by the structure there is an oak-paneled, 1238-seat auditorium and below it, a 200-seat theater.

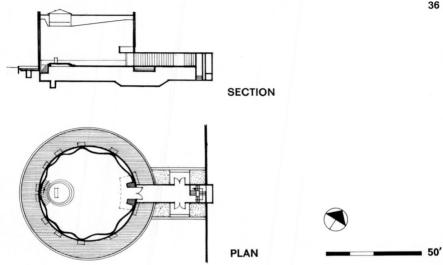

SECTION

PLAN

50'

M.I.T. Chapel   **1955**
West Campus, Massachusetts Avenue   **Cambridge**
architect: Eero Saarinen; associate architects: Anderson, Beckwith and Haible

The nondenominational chapel seats 130, but it is also designed for individual meditation. Its undulating interior wall improves the building's acoustics while providing space for ventilating ducts. Daylight is reflected on the wall from below by a surrounding moat and also enters directly in one dramatic shaft from a skylight above the altar. The altar screen is by Harry Bertoia, the spire and bell by Theodore Rozak.

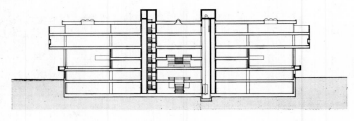

READING ROOM
OFFICE FLOOR
MEZZANINE
MAIN FLOOR
GROUND FLOOR
BASEMENT

SECTION

■■■■■■ **100′**

M.I.T. Julius Adams Stratton Building   **1965**
West Campus, Massachusetts Avenue   **Cambridge**
architect: Eduardo Catalano; associate architects: Brannen & Shimamoto

Diverse, nonacademic, student facilities are efficiently organized within this 190,000 square foot building. One large, central stair connects the shops in the basement with those on the ground floor, and another links social and dining facilities on the main floor and mezzanine. The careful finish of its cast-in-place concrete structure and skin helps to make the powerful building compatible with the limestone-faced M.I.T. buildings across the street.

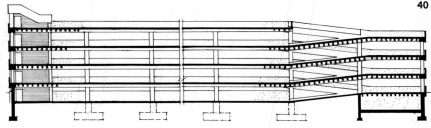

SECTION

50'

M.I.T. West Parking Facility
West Campus, Vassar Street

1964
Cambridge

architect: Parking Development Company; associate architect: Marvin E. Goody & John M. Clancy, Inc.

Located on a narrow strip of land along the northern border of the M.I.T. Campus, this strongly horizontal, roughly finished, service building forms a wall along that border and a backdrop for the expanse of playing fields to the South. Its concrete frame was poured in place around precast double T beams, thus creating a rigid structure. Precast railing panels are clipped to the outside of the frame.

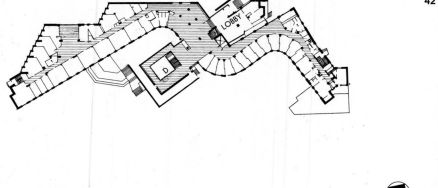

100'

M.I.T. Baker House Dormitory
West Campus, 362 Memorial Drive

1949
Cambridge

architect: Alvar Aalto; associate architects: Perry, Shaw, Hepburn and Dean

The daring curvilinear shape of this building takes maximum advantage of the view by increasing the perimeter exposed to the river. This curve also visually shortens the corridors and produces an interesting variety of sizes and shapes for the individual rooms. The unusually dark and irregular brick on the exterior creates a rich and lively texture.

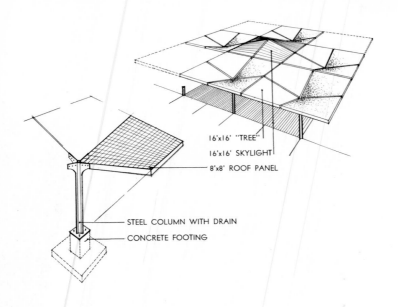

16'x16' "TREE"

16'x16' SKYLIGHT

8'x8' ROOF PANEL

STEEL COLUMN WITH DRAIN

CONCRETE FOOTING

1961
Cambridge

Experimental School
79 Moore Street
architects: M.I.T. Departments of Architecture and Civil Engineering

This is a prototype structure illustrating a wholly prefabricated system for the design and construction of schools. It is the product of research sponsored by the Educational Facilities Laboratories to find a quickly constructed schoolhouse of high quality that would allow flexibility of planning and design. The basic unit is a 16' square, bolted together, hyperbolic paraboloid "tree." Four of these units plus a skylight form a classroom. They can be assembled in a variety of plans to suit specific school district's needs and then can be easily moved or rearranged as these needs change.

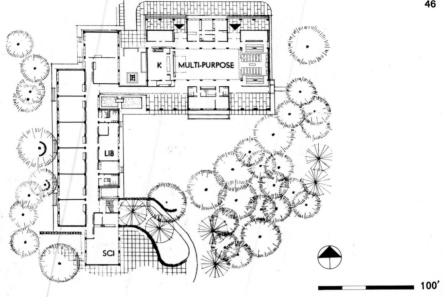

Maimonides School
Philbrick Road

1961
Brookline

architect: Hugh Stubbins & Associates, Inc.

This private parochial school is on a well-wooded estate in an established residential area. The old wall surrounding the property remains, and the roof of the school rises behind it in a series of small barrel vaults. Preservation of the residential quality and scale in the architecture and the landscaping creates an environment appropriate to both the building's use and its neighborhood.

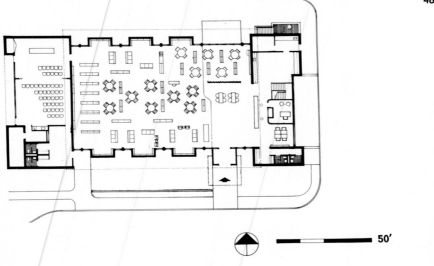

50′

Putterham Branch Library
959 West Roxbury Parkway

1962
Brookline

architect: The Architects Collaborative; Jean Fletcher, partner in charge

The low brick walls of this branch library help relate it to the surrounding residential neighborhood. A community meeting room and an enclosed work area flank its one large, high-ceilinged reading room, which can be supervised from a single desk. The room is subdivided into children's, young peoples', and adults' areas by furniture groupings. Book alcoves, set in the glass perimeter wall, provide a focus for each small group and limit glare in the open room.

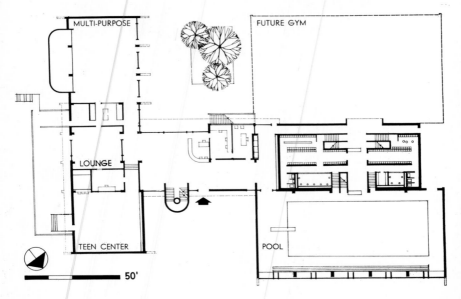

MULTI-PURPOSE

FUTURE GYM

LOUNGE

TEEN CENTER

POOL

50'

Washington Park YMCA   **1965**
Warren Street and Washington Park Boulevard   **Roxbury**
architect: The Architects Collaborative; Norman Fletcher, partner in charge

This building is designed to be the focus for a community of about 4000 in what is now Boston's most depressed area. Although security dictated a fairly closed building at the street level, where all rooms open to fenced courtyards or patios, an attempt was made to orient the second floor outward to the neighborhood. The placement of a sculptured concrete wall at the entry helps to make the building more inviting to the passerby; and a prominent stair tower, topped by a music listening room, is a symbol of the surrounding community of the Y's special role there.

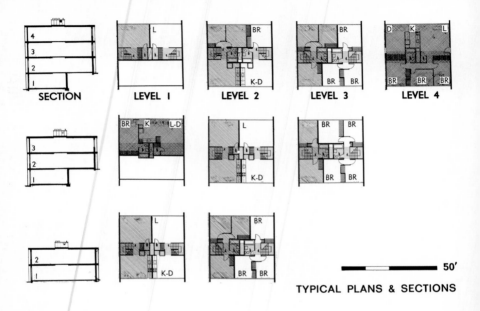

SECTION   **LEVEL 1**   **LEVEL 2**   **LEVEL 3**   **LEVEL 4**

50'

TYPICAL PLANS & SECTIONS

Academy Homes
Columbus Avenue and Ritchie Street
architect: Carl Koch & Associates, Inc.

1965
Roxbury

The building system used for this moderate-priced development for 202 families was designed in a housing study commissioned by the Boston Redevelopment Authority. It employs precast, prestressed concrete panels spanning 32' between bearing walls. The 32' module allows several apartment plans (from 1 to 4 bedrooms). The units are stacked from 2 to 4 stories high and arranged to form a variety of spaces on the 7-acre site.

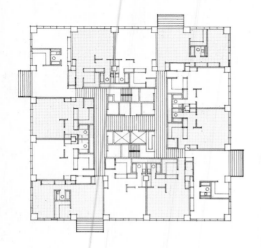

50'

Charlesbank Apartments
650 Huntington Avenue
architect: Hugh Stubbins & Associates, Inc.

1963
Roxbury

Efficient planning makes the most of the space within this building's 276 small apartments. The equally compact arrangement of the apartments around the central elevators and stairs avoids long corridors, and the square pinwheel plan results in four identical elevations for the 24-story tower. The orderly facades are composed of precast concrete panels alternating with aluminum sash designed to accommodate individual air-conditioning units.

SPECIAL
FACILITIES

BOOKS AND
MONOGRAPHS

ENTRY

JOURNALS
AND INDICES

SECTION

50'

Harvard Francis A. Countway Library of Medicine
Harvard Medical School, Shattuck Street
architect: Hugh Stubbins & Associates, Inc.

1965
Roxbury

Located among the monumental, neoclassic buildings of Harvard Medical School, the library acknowledges its surroundings with its symmetrical form, its limestone facing, and its apparently deep cornice, which is really a full floor of offices. The main entry is by bridge over a dry moat that brings light to the 2 floors below. A central, skylit court is the focus of the inward-oriented building. The perimeter walls of the 3 floors, containing books and monographs, are mostly solid, and the small glass areas are shielded to avoid glare.

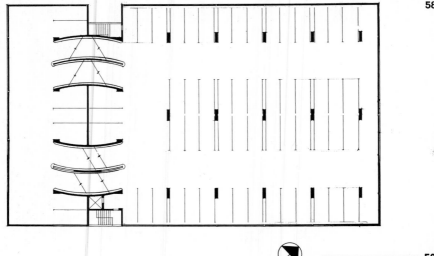

50′

Children's Hospital Parking Facility
Longwood Avenue and Binney Street
architect: The Architects Collaborative; John C. Harkness, partner in charge

1964
Roxbury

This compact garage contains 165,000 square feet on seven split levels. It can house 457 cars with self-service parking and 652 cars if attendants are employed, as is currently the case. The well-detailed structure is cast-in-place concrete with a post-tensioned grid slab to permit the large corner cantilevers. The railing panels are precast and are set within the frame.

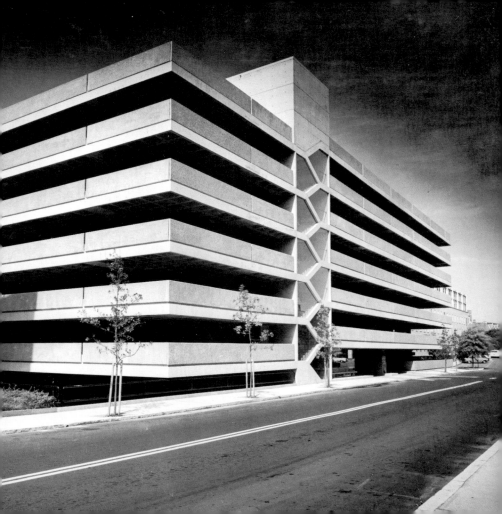

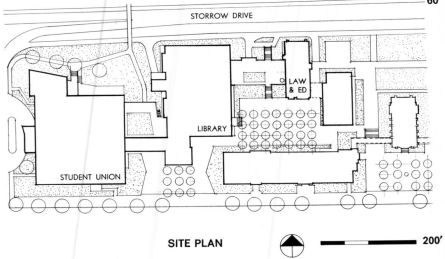

STORROW DRIVE

LAW & ED

LIBRARY

STUDENT UNION

SITE PLAN

200'

Boston University Schools of Law and Education
765 Commonwealth Avenue

1963
Boston

architects: Sert, Jackson and Gourley in association with Edwin T. Steffian

This 22-story tower takes advantage of its location on a bend in the Charles River, where its strong silhouette is seen from different points along the curving river drive and is an exciting addition to the Boston skyline. The upper stories house the School of Education and the lower, together with an adjacent law library, house the School of Law. The building is part of a well-planned complex by the same architect that also includes a student union, a central library, and a series of plazas formed both by the new and the existing structures.

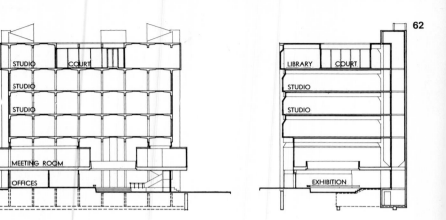

LONGITUDINAL SECTION

LATERAL SECTION

■━━━━ 50'

Boston Architectural Center
320 Newbury Street
architect: Ashley, Myer & Associates, Inc.

196–
Boston

The design for this architectural school and center was chosen by means of a competition won by the principals of this firm with William L. Hall, Robert Goodman, Robert L. O'Nell, and Richard I. Krauss. The building selected is free standing on three sides, with stairs and utilities grouped along the one party wall, and a clear span across the remaining area. This leaves large, flexible spaces for the studios, meeting room, and exhibitions.

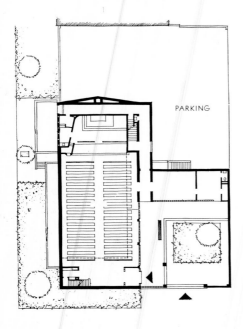

PARKING

50'

First Lutheran Church
299 Berkeley Street
architect: Pietro Belluschi

1959
Boston

Located on a busy street, the church is entered through a quiet courtyard and a porch, which comfortably make the transition to the restrained, dignified sanctuary. The brick cavity walls are exposed on the interior with the exception of a wood slat screen around the lower altar area, an acoustical aid in the generally hard-surfaced hall.

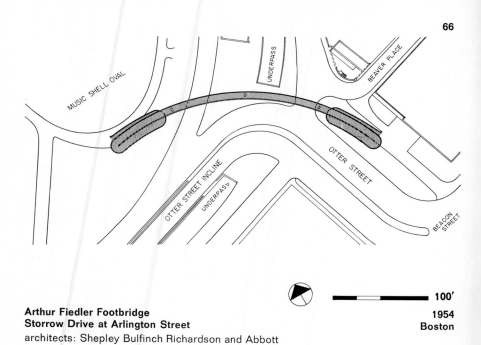

Arthur Fiedler Footbridge
Storrow Drive at Arlington Street
architects: Shepley Bulfinch Richardson and Abbott

100'
1954
Boston

Linking the Back Bay residential area with the Esplanade, the footbridge is used periodically by large numbers of people attending outdoor concerts along the river as well as daily by strollers, often with baby carriages, and by bicyclists. The 92' spanning girders of the reinforced-concrete structure are utilized as guard rails, thus lowering the walkway and reducing the pedestrians' climb. The circuitous walk across the drive is one of constantly changing views from different heights, directions, and degrees of enclosure.

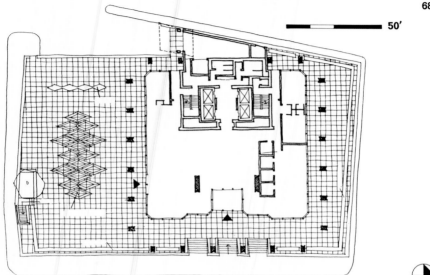

50'

Blue Cross – Blue Shield Building
133 Federal Street
architects: Anderson Beckwith and Haible, and Paul Rudolph

1960
Boston

In this single-occupancy office building, the air-conditioning ducts as well as the columns are incorporated in the vertical elements of the precast-concrete facade. The only interior supports are two large columns and the structural elevator core, leaving most of the 7400 square feet of work space per floor unobstructed. There is a skylit cafeteria in the raised podium on which the building sits.

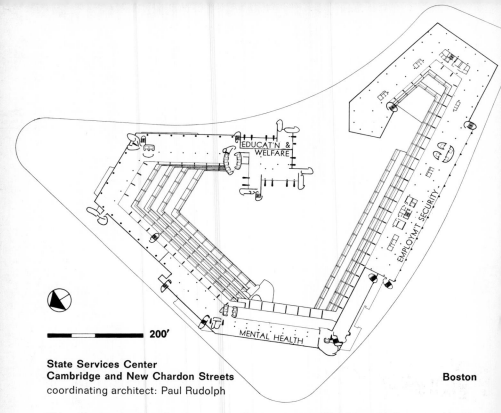

State Services Center
Cambridge and New Chardon Streets   **Boston**
coordinating architect: Paul Rudolph

This complex houses three separate State services (Employment Security; Health, Education and Welfare; and Mental Health) in three buildings designed by three different architectural offices (Shepley Bulfinch Richardson and Abbot; M. A. Dyer and Pedersen and Tilney; and Desmond & Lord, Inc.). They have been coordinated into one superblock around a large plaza enclosing a lively multilevel space.

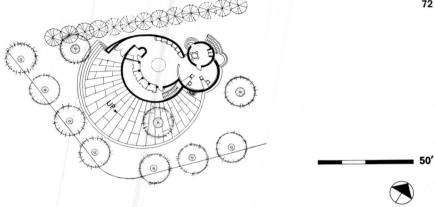

50'

National Shawmut Branch Bank   **1963**
109 Cambridge Street   **Boston**
architects: Imre and Anthony Halasz; associate architect: Marvin E. Goody & John M.
        Clancy, Inc.

The site of this small branch bank is a corner in the Government Center area, surrounded by large office buildings. Unable to compete with its tall neighbors, the tiny
building is designed as a pavilion with no elements suggestive of relative scale: the
door is deeply recessed, and light enters from the skylights. The resulting snug form
is particularly appropriate for a bank.

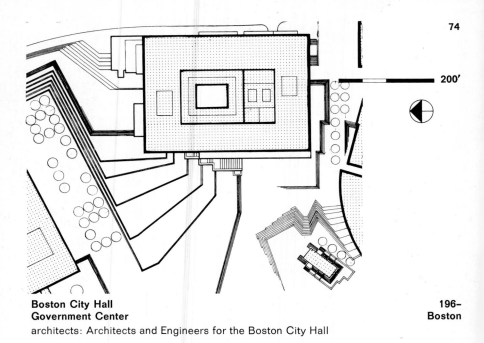

**Boston City Hall
Government Center**
architects: Architects and Engineers for the Boston City Hall

The City Hall and its surrounding sculptured plaza are constructed from the winning design submitted by Gerhard M. Kallmann, Noel M. McKinnell, and Edward F. Knowles in an architectural competition held in 1962. Its comparatively low height is the result of a limitation set with the aim of distinguishing it from the tall State, Federal, and commercial office buildings surrounding the new Government Center. The three major types of spaces in the City Hall are separated horizontally with offices on the top three floors, ceremonial spaces in the middle, and departments receiving many visitors in the broad brick base.

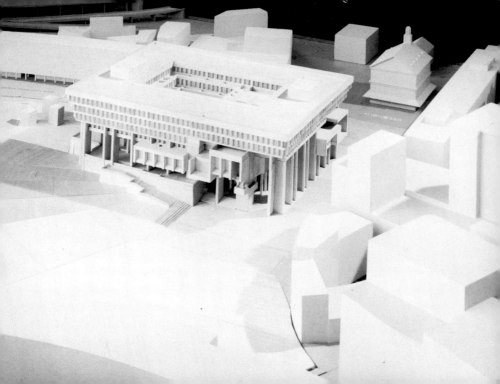

ENVIRONS

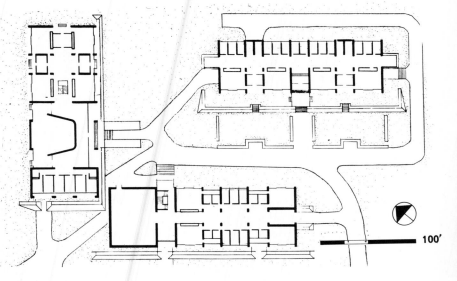

100'

**Academic Quadrangle
Brandeis University**

1959
Waltham

architect: The Architects Collaborative; Benjamin Thompson, partner in charge

The three buildings forming this group are set on the crest of one of the rolling hills of the Brandeis campus. Similar in function, but not identical, each contains a different arrangement of classrooms, offices, and lecture hall. A common structural bay size, clearly expressed by the exposed concrete frames, orders and unifies the group. The strong, horizontal lines of monolithic stone retaining walls and heavy cornices contribute to this unity and to the quiet dignity of the space enclosed by the buildings.

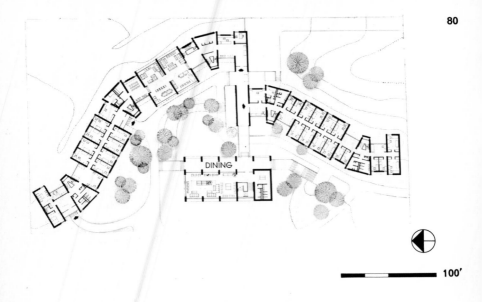

DINING

100'

East Quadrangle Dormitories
Brandeis University

1963
Waltham

architect: The Architects Collaborative; Benjamin Thompson, partner in charge

Triangular stair towers join rectangular blocks of sleeping and study rooms to allow this building to curve with the contours of the hill into which it is set. The brick bearing walls are exposed on the interior, as is the concrete grid slab ceiling. Rooms are grouped — 4 doubles and 2 singles — about a study, with shared bath facilities near the stairs.

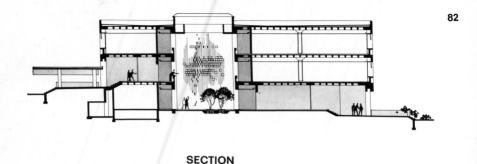

SECTION

50′

Offices   1963
275 Wyman Street   Waltham
architects: Anderson, Beckwith and Haible

All entries and corridors lead to the skylit court which provides a focus for this multiple-tenancy office building. Camellias, a planting bed, and a pool are set in the quarry tile floor of the court. A copper sheet and rod mural by Michio Ihara presents changing patterns as one walks around the surrounding balconies and as the natural light varies during the course of the day.

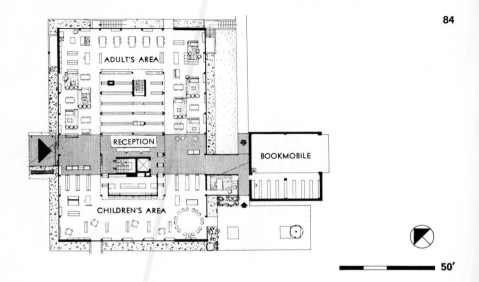

ADULT'S AREA

RECEPTION

BOOKMOBILE

CHILDREN'S AREA

50'

Wellesley Free Library
530 Washington Street
architect: Carl Koch & Associates, Inc.

1959
Wellesley

Dormer windows in the hip roof of the library bring natural light into the three-level core of stacks. The perimeter reading areas receive light from large windows which go to the floor. Between these glass areas are porcelain enamel panels in rich colors, designed by Gyorgy Kepes. The doors to the library, also in porcelain enamel, are by Juliet Kepes.

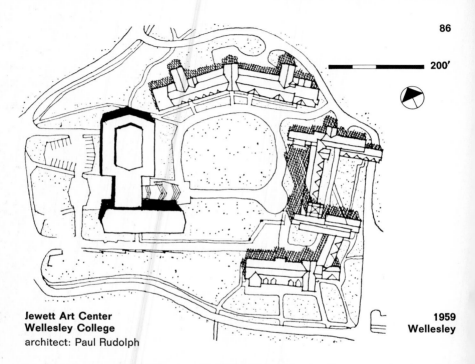

200'

Jewett Art Center
Wellesley College
architect: Paul Rudolph

1959
Wellesley

Located near several existing neo-Gothic buildings, the Art Center is related to them not only by its scale, silhouette, and materials but also by its massing and placement to enclose a large plaza with them. The articulation of the building in three distinct volumes enables it to create a corner of this new quadrangle as well as an entrance to it. The south and west sides of this corner are formed by the visual arts and performing arts wings, respectively, while a second-floor gallery bridges between them and spans the elaborate entry stairs to the new plaza.

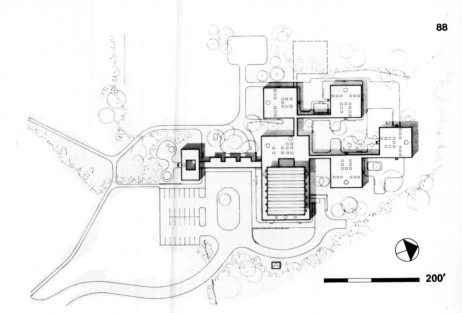

200'

Hanscom Elementary School
L. G. Hanscom Field

1960
Lincoln

architect: The Architects Collaborative; Louis A. McMillen, partner in charge

Independently heated clusters of 4 classrooms, each with adjacent outdoor play space, help give an appropriately small scale to this elementary school, as well as simplify expansion and/or partial use. The building is located on the site (which was farmland in the nineteenth century) to take advantage of the old stone walls and the second-growth trees.

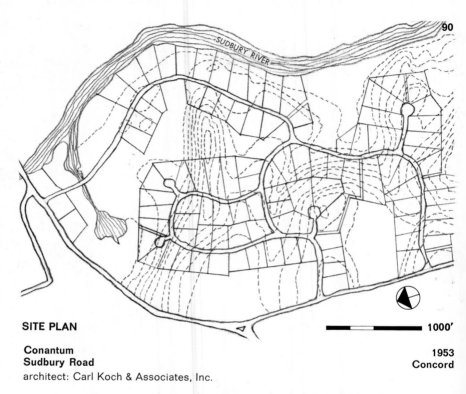

SITE PLAN

1000′

Conantum
Sudbury Road
architect: Carl Koch & Associates, Inc.

1953
Concord

This suburban development of 100 homes (built from standard elements with slight variations in plan) is laid out along curving roads that follow the topography. Careful preservation of the woods in which the houses are skillfully sited gives a high degree of privacy and individuality to the 1-acre lots.

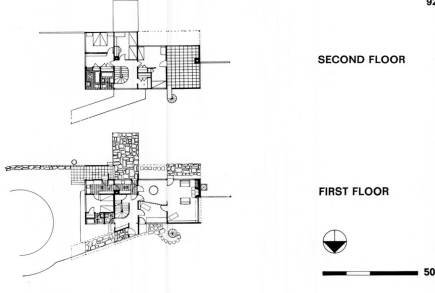

SECOND FLOOR

FIRST FLOOR

50'

Gropius Residence
Baker Bridge Road
architects: Walter Gropius and Marcel Breuer

1937
Lincoln

Built soon after his arrival in this country, Gropius' residence combines commonly used materials in an unconventional manner to produce a house suitable both for its environment and its inhabitants' way of life. The light wood framing and white painted siding are familiar to the area, but unlike the traditional cellular, New England residence, there is an easy flow of space both within the house and from the interior to the exterior.

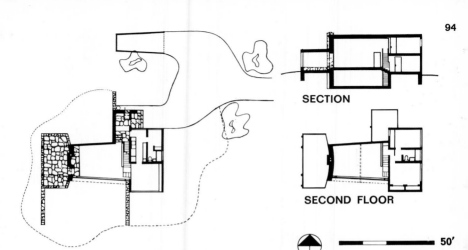

SECTION

SECOND FLOOR

50'

Breuer Residence
Woods End Road

1938
Lincoln

architects: Walter Gropius and Marcel Breuer

Like the Gropius residence, Breuer's bachelor cottage uses local materials and features in a new form appropriate for the area and the occupant. Fieldstone is prominent both in the base of the porch and in the large, curved fireplace wall. This sculptural wall dominates the living room which, because of the split level plan, is almost two stories high. The placement of the stairs along one side of and open to the room permits enjoyment of the space from many levels and views.

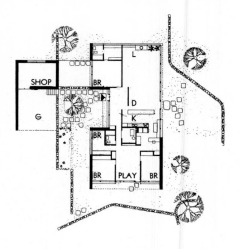

50'

Laaff Residence
Reservation Road
architects: Marcel Breuer and Associates

1957
Andover

Built almost 20 years after his own house in Lincoln, this residence by Breuer is similar in its effective use of local stone. Except for large glass areas, all exterior walls are stone, whitewashed in some places. Stone walls of varying heights are also important elements in the landscaping and help to join the clean-lined house with its hilltop site.

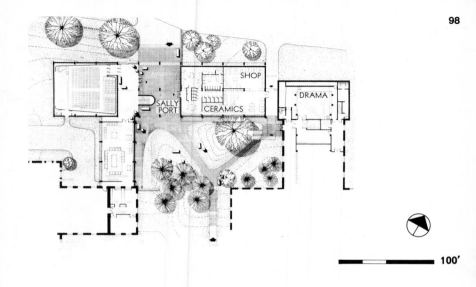

Arts and Communications Building
Phillips Academy

1963
Andover

architect: The Architects Collaborative; Benjamin Thompson, partner in charge

The most prominent of several excellent buildings recently added to the neo-Georgian campus of this boys' school, the Art Center joins two existing buildings and creates a major entrance to the whole campus. Consideration was given to the older buildings in the proportion of column to cornice and in choice of materials: brick to match that existing and bushhammered concrete similar in texture to the old granite.

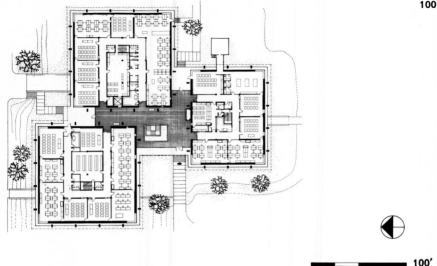

Science Building　　　　　　　　　　　　　　　　　　**1963**
Phillips Academy　　　　　　　　　　　　　　　　　　**Andover**
architect: The Architects Collaborative; Benjamin Thompson, partner in charge

The Science Building uses the same carefully detailed materials as the Art Center.
They are exposed on the interior, as is the grid slab ceiling, and complemented by the
wood paneling in the corridors and a slate floor in the lobby. The Chemistry, Physics,
and Biology Departments are each housed in one of the three units clustered around
the lobby.

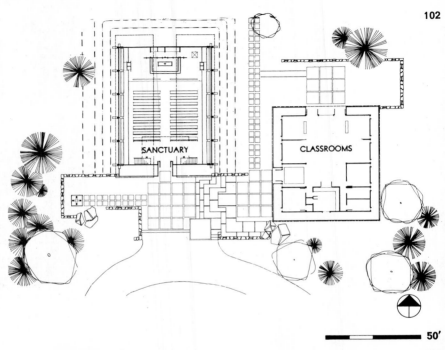

SANCTUARY

CLASSROOMS

50'

Mt. Calvary Lutheran Church
472 Massachusetts Avenue
architect: Joseph Schiffer

1963
Acton

The strong form of this country church is emphasized by dramatic lighting from roof skylights between the curved walls. A small building (seating about 200), its finish materials are limited to red cedar for the decking, siding, and shingles.

APPENDIX

MAP I   BOSTON

MAP II ENVIRONS

SOURCE OF PHOTOGRAPHS

Arber French & Co., Inc.	First Lutheran Church
Nishan Bicharjian	Boston City Hall
Creative Photographers, Inc.	Conantum
George Cserna	M.I.T. Cecil and Ida Green Building
G. M. Cushing, Jr.	Arthur Fiedler Footbridge Siple Residence
Gottscho-Schleisner, Inc.	Harvard Quincy House
Robert F. Haiko	M.I.T. Julius Adams Stratton Building
Harvard News Service	Harvard Carpenter Center for the Visual Arts Harvard Graduate School of Education Harvard Married Student Housing, Peabody Terrace
David Hirsch	Maimonides School Peabody School
Clemens Kalischer	Blue Cross - Blue Shield Building Harvard Loeb Drama Center
Phokion Karas	Academy Homes Boston Architectural Center Boston University Schools of Law and Education Children's Hospital Parking Facility M.I.T. West Parking Facility Tufts Library
Balthazar Korab	National Shawmut Branch Bank
Alessandro Macone, Inc.	Mt. Calvary Lutheran Church
M.I.T. News Service	M.I.T. Baker House Dormitory M.I.T. Chapel

Lucia Moholy-Nagy	Gropius Residence
Joseph W. Molitor	Charlesbank Apartments
	Jewett Art Center: Wellesley College
Louis Reens	East Quadrangle Dormitories: Brandeis University
	Hanscom Elementary School
	Harvard Francis A. Countway Library of Medicine
	Harvard Holyoke Center
	Residence, 1 Mt. Pleasant
	NEGEA Service Corporation
	Putterham Branch Library
	Sert Residence
	Washington Park YMCA
Ben Schnall	Laaff Residence
Julius Shulman	Arts and Communications Building: Phillips Academy
Ezra Stoller	Academic Quadrangle: Brandeis University
	Breuer Residence
	Eastgate Apartments
	M.I.T. Kresge Auditorium
	Science Building: Phillips Academy
	State Services Center
	Wellesley Free Library
Fred Stone, Inc.	Harvard Graduate Center
	Offices, 275 Wyman Street
Cover photograph	Model of the Seal of Boston from the War Memorial Auditorium.
	Architects: Hoyle, Doran and Berry.
	Sculptor: Arcangelo Cascieri

INDEX